Student Guide t

Contents

INTRODUCTION 2
LOGIN AND EXITING PROCEDURES 2
THE BLACKBOARD ENVIRONMENT 4
    The Main Course Window 4
    Navigation Area 4
    Control Buttons 5
COURSE MATERIALS 6
    Accessing Linked Files 6
    Accessing and Taking Assessments 7
    Answering Questions 7
    Submitting Answers for Grading 7
    Reviewing Assessment Results 8
COMMUNICATION TOOLS 9
    Send E-Mail 9
    Roster 10
    Group Pages 11
    Virtual Classroom 11
    Discussion Board 13
STUDENT TOOLS 20
    Digital Drop Box 21
    Edit Your Homepage 23
    Personal Information 24
    Course Calendar 27
    Check Grade 29
    Manual 29
    Tasks 29
    Electric Blackboard 30
    Address Book 31
SUCCESSFUL USE OF THE STUDENT GUIDE TO BLACKBOARD 32

Student Guide to Blackboard

INTRODUCTION

Welcome to the *Student Guide to Blackboard*. This guide will direct you through the navigation, features, and functionality of your Blackboard course. This student guide was written for Blackboard Version 5. If your version of Blackboard is earlier than version 5, please go to *http://www.course.com/onlinecontent/blackboard/student/ckversion.cfm* to obtain student instructions specific to the version of Blackboard you are using.

This guide is divided into six sections:

- Enrolling and Entering Courses
- The Blackboard Environment
- Navigating in a Course
- Course Materials
- Communication Tools
- Student Tools

Each section includes a general description of the area and step-by-step instructions to perform appropriate tasks. While you are enrolling and taking your course online, you will need access to:

- An Internet connection
- A Web browser - Netscape 4.01 (or higher) or Internet Explorer 4.0 (or higher)
- An e-mail account

LOGIN AND EXITING PROCEDURES

Once you have enrolled into a course, you can enter and exit the course anytime.

Entering a Course

1. Direct your browser to the course URL provided by your instructor. The entry page should look similar to Figure 1a.
2. Click the Login button.
3. Type your username and password in the appropriate boxes. Click the login button (Figure 1b).

LOGIN AND EXITING PROCEDURES

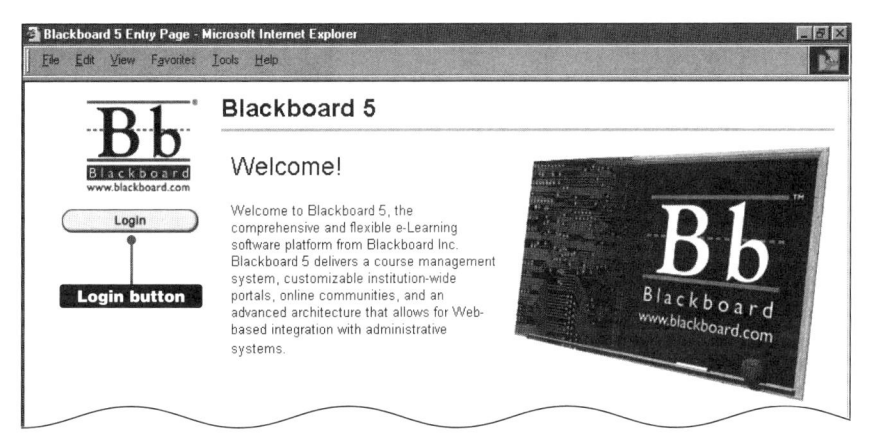

FIGURE 1a

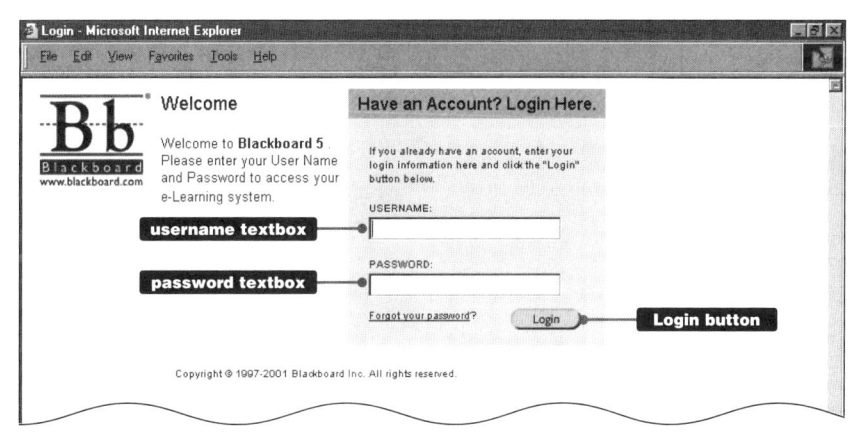

FIGURE 1b

Exiting a Course

1. Click the Logout link (Figure 2) and then close your browser.

You can enter and exit a course area by using the navigation buttons located in the navigation area. To enter a course area, click the appropriate button in the navigation area. Some of these buttons may not be available if your instructor has disabled an area.

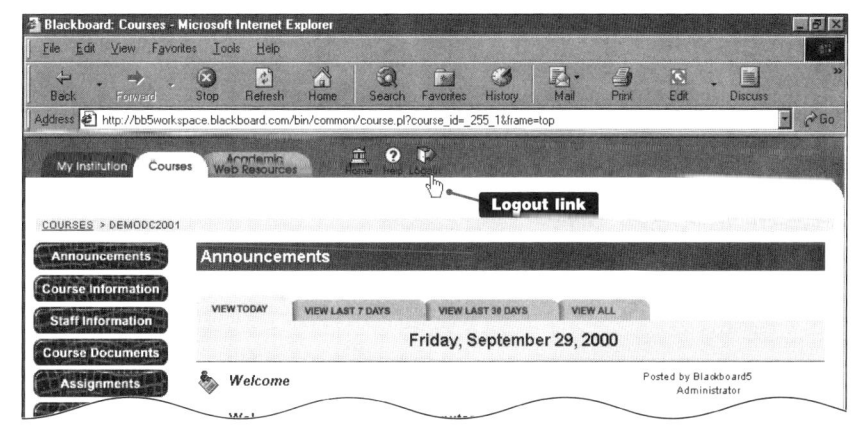

FIGURE 2

STUDENT GUIDE TO BLACKBOARD

THE BLACKBOARD ENVIRONMENT

When you log in to your course, you will enter the Course Site. The Course Site consists of three main components: the main course window, the navigation area, and the control buttons.

The Main Course Window

The **main course window** should be considered your home screen (Figure 3). When using Blackboard, all content and communication tools display in this area. Announcements can be found on this page every time you log in to the course. Pertinent information regarding course assignments, discussion topics, and even exams may be displayed in the Announcements section.

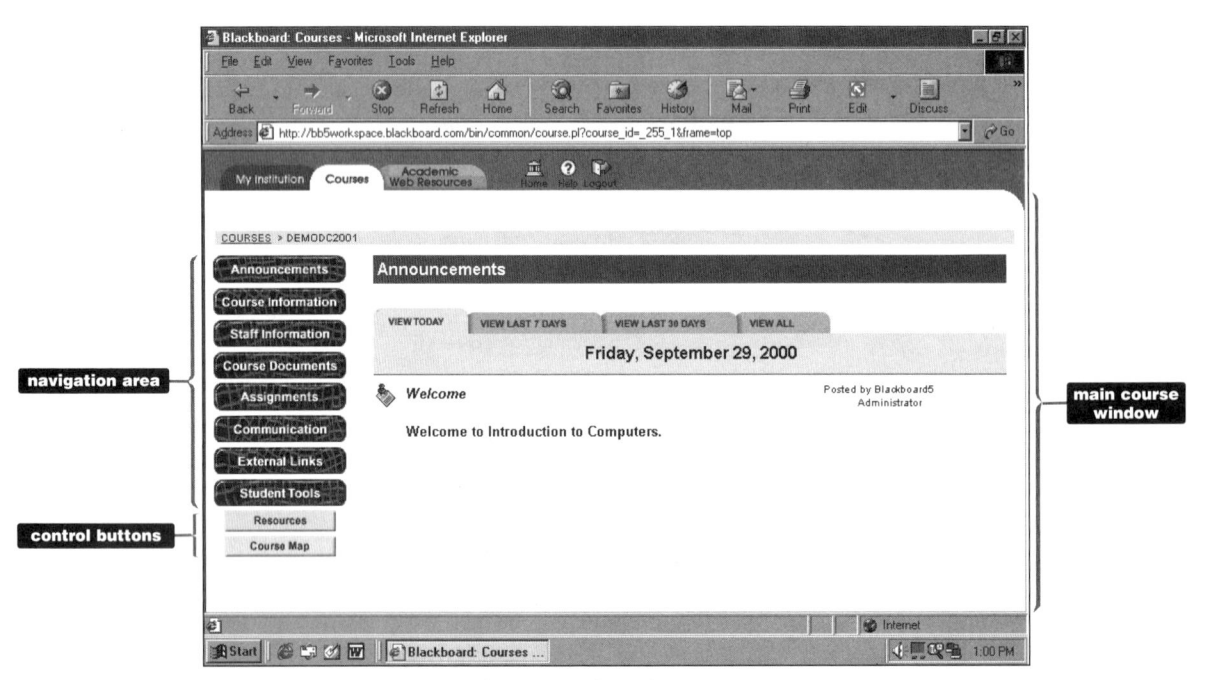

FIGURE 3

Navigation Area

The **navigation area** consists of a row of buttons located along the left side of the window. Clicking any of these buttons in the navigation area will take you to the corresponding area of the course. Certain areas may be secure, or password protected, to ensure that only registered students can enter and to keep grading information private between students and instructors. Table 1 on the next page lists some of the commonly used course buttons in the navigation area and specifies their function. The course buttons in your course may differ slightly from those listed in Table 1.

Control Buttons

Two **control buttons**, located below the navigation area, guide you through the course. The **Resources button** links directly to Blackboard online resources to assist with course-related issues. The **Course Map button** allows you easy access to Course Information, Staff Information, Course Documents, Assignments, Communication, External Links, and Student Tools. This function is available only in Internet Explorer 4.0 or Netscape 4.01 or higher browsers.

Navigating Using the Course Map Button

1. Click the Course Map button in the control buttons area.
2. When the small Course Contents window displays in the Blackboard window, click the book icon next to the section you would like to enter (Figure 4 on the next page).
3. The contents of the section display as links. Click the desired link (Figure 5 on the next page).

The link will open in the course page.

Table 1 Navigation Area Buttons

BUTTON	FUNCTION
Announcements	Displays announcements, updates, and reminders. Announcements display in the main course window each time you enter the course.
Course Information	Displays general information about the course, which may include approved course descriptions, a listing of prerequisites, a course syllabus, and times/locations for lecture components.
Staff Information	Contains specific information about staff or faculty who are involved in the course.
Course Documents	Contains the majority of information that will be delivered online, such as course outlines, handouts, lecture materials, related readings and links, and practice quizzes.
Assignments	Consists of course assignments, tests, quizzes, and surveys.
Communication	Includes all the communication tools needed for the discussion board, chat, e-mail, student and group pages, and the student roster.
External Links	Lists helpful URLs you can use to take virtual field trips or view-related course material.
Student Tools	Includes all the student tools needed to submit information to your instructor, view a course calendar, check your grades, manage your homepage, and edit your profile.

COURSE MATERIALS

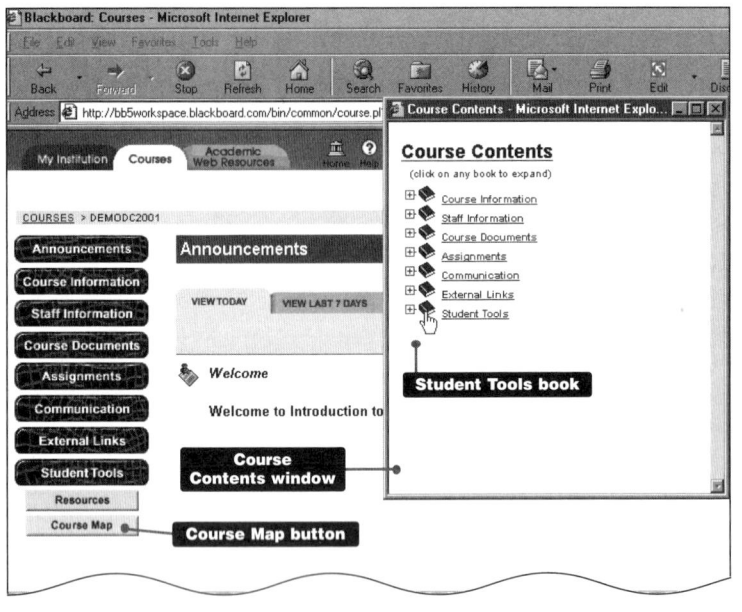

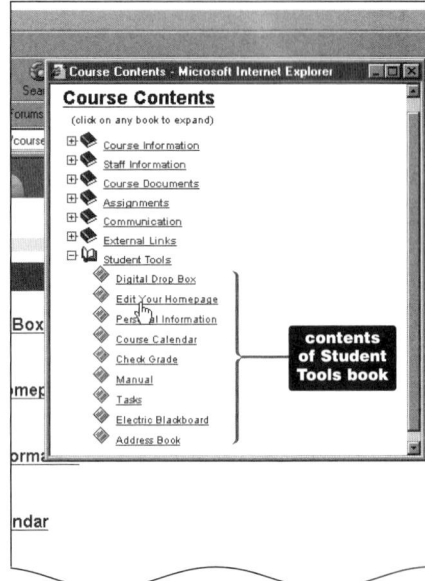

FIGURE 4

FIGURE 5

COURSE MATERIALS

Using the navigation buttons, you can access all course materials. The course materials can be in several different formats, including HTML, text, audio, video, and Word documents.

Accessing Linked Files

An instructor can attach a file to course material. When a file is attached, it displays as a link (Figure 6). You must click the link to access the information. Depending on your computer configuration, how the file was linked, and the type of file, several things may happen when you click a link. The link may open in the main course window. The link may open in a new browser window. The link may prompt you with a dialog box, asking if you want to save the file to a local drive. The link may ask if you want to open it without saving. The link may launch a different program (such as Microsoft Word) and display the file.

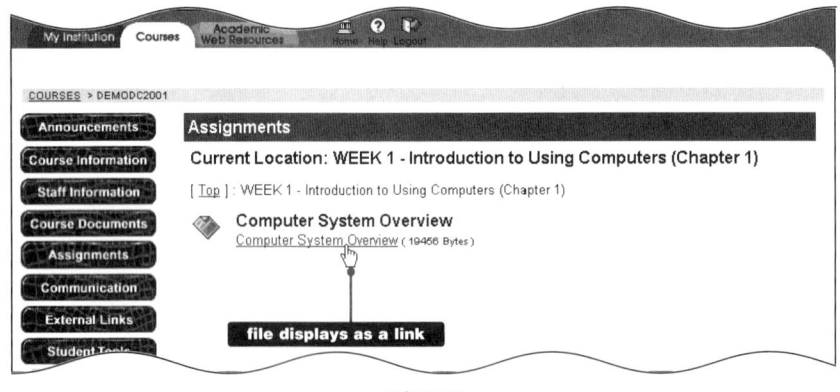

FIGURE 6

COURSE MATERIALS

Accessing and Taking Assessments

Blackboard contains an assessment feature that delivers tests, quizzes, practice questions, and surveys to students. If your instructor decides to use this tool, you will be expected to enter, take, and submit the assessment. The Instructor may set the quiz to be timed. The quiz environment appears in the bottom left corner of the browser.

Sometimes an instructor will post an announcement that informs students about the assessment. This announcement will have a link that takes you directly to the assessment. If no announcement exists, the assessment may be located within a Course Information, Course Documents, Assignments, or Books page. The Books course button is not shown in the figures in this manual.

Taking an Assessment

1. Click the assessment link on the Announcement page.

    OR

1. Locate the appropriate course area. The assessment is included in Assignments, Course Documents, Course Information, or Books.
2. Click the Take quiz link below the appropriate quiz to begin (Figure 7).
3. When the confirmation dialogue box displays, click the OK button (Figure 8).

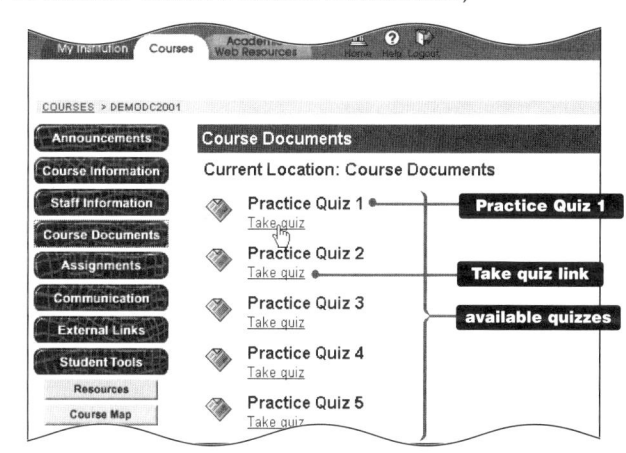

FIGURE 7

Answering Questions

Several different types of questions are available that instructors can include in assessments. These include multiple choice, true/false, fill-in-the-blank, multiple answer, matching, ordering, and short answer/essay. Except for the short answer/essay questions, all answers are graded automatically and the results are submitted into the online gradebook. Short answer/essay questions are graded by instructors, graders, or teachers' assistants and then manually entered into the gradebook. For more information about the type and format of questions in an assessment, refer to the online Student Manual. To view the Student Manual, click the Student Tools button in the navigation area and then click Manual.

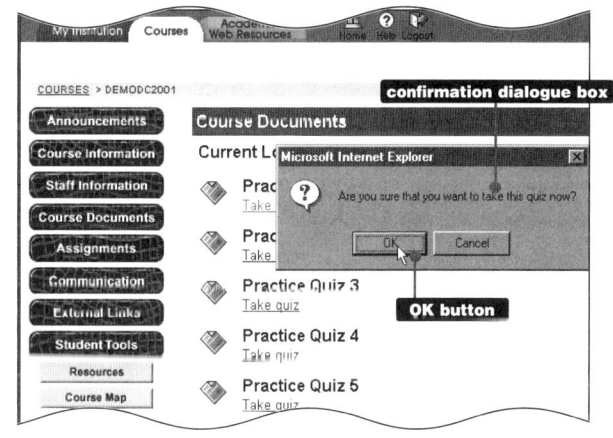

FIGURE 8

Submitting Answers for Grading

When you have finished answering the questions in your assessment, you must submit the answers. The assessments are submitted into Blackboard according to the

STUDENT GUIDE TO BLACKBOARD | 7

COURSE MATERIALS

options selected by the instructor. If the assessment is a test or a quiz, your answers will be assessed and a grade will be recorded into the gradebook. If the assessment requires manual grading (essay questions), the gradebook will report that you completed the assessment, but the grade will not display until your essays have been evaluated. If the assessment is a survey, your answers will be recorded anonymously, but the gradebook will report that you have completed the survey. There is no "Saved Assessment." The student must click the Submit button before the quiz will go to the gradebook.

Submitting an Assessment

1. Click the Submit button at the end of the assessment (Figure 9).

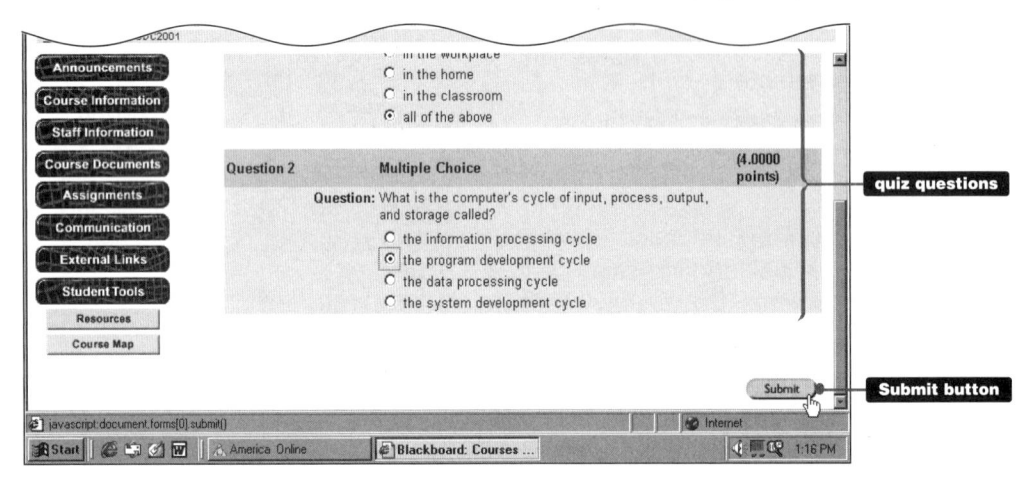

FIGURE 9

Reviewing Assessment Results

The instructor can permit students to view certain results after submitting an assessment. These include seeing the question and your answer, seeing the correct answer, and seeing feedback/remediation for the question. An example of assessment results with feedback is shown in Figure 10.

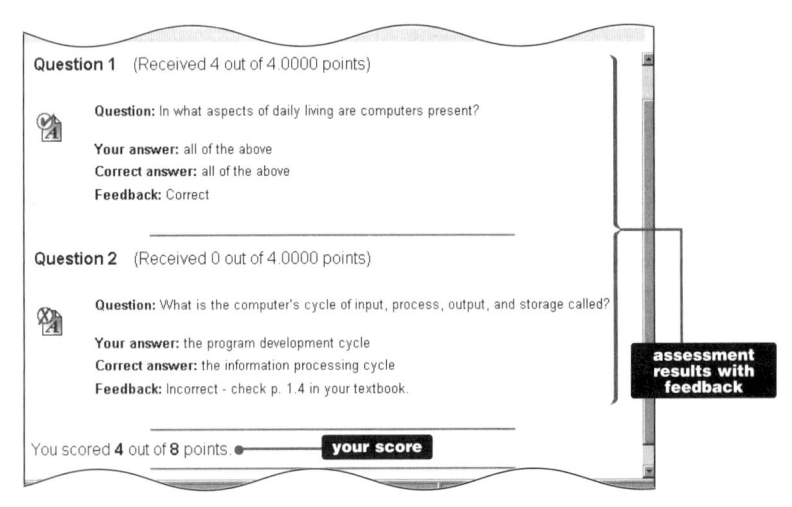

FIGURE 10

Instructors can determine which of the result options you see. They can choose to reveal or not to reveal any of these items. If the instructor chooses not to reveal any of these items, you simply may receive a tally of your raw score compared with the total amount of points possible (Figure 11).

Remember, viewing assessment results is different from viewing your course grades. For information about the online gradebook, see the Student Tools section of this manual.

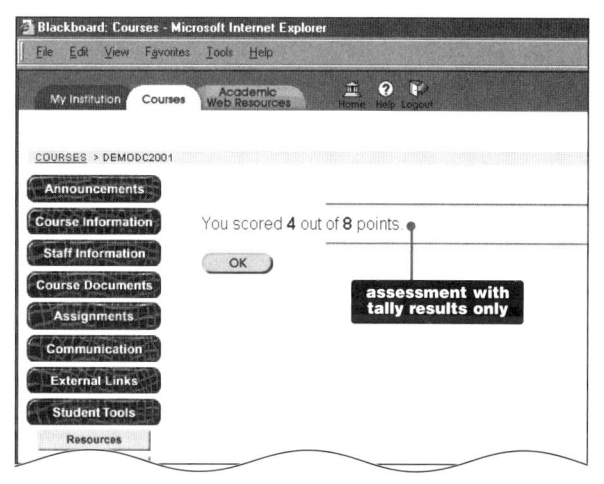

FIGURE 11

COMMUNICATION TOOLS

Blackboard offers full-service communication tools to class participants (Figure 12). Within this area, instructors and students can contact each other via e-mail, conduct a chat, participate in a discussion, and work in groups. Students also can utilize these features to view the student roster and student homepages. All of these options may not be available if your instructor has disabled them.

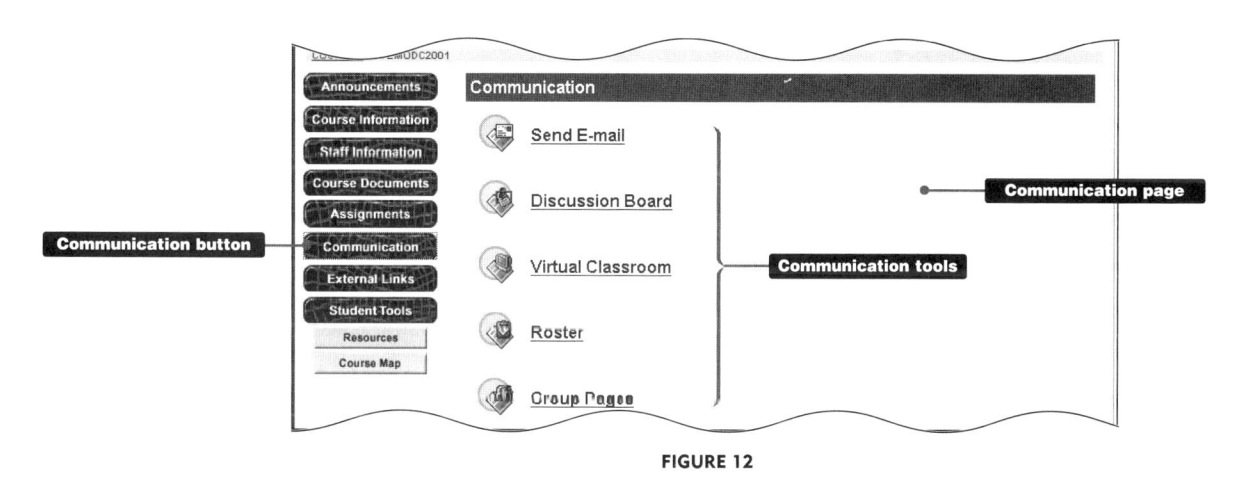

FIGURE 12

Send E-Mail

The **e-mail** function was developed to provide a quick method of contacting course participants. From the Send E-mail page, you can send e-mail to anyone in the course. However, Blackboard is not where you read responses to the e-mails sent by you. Students must open their e-mail program to view all responses.

COMMUNICATION TOOLS

Sending E-Mail

1. Click the Communication button in the navigation area and then click Send E-Mail (see Figure 12 on the previous page).
2. Select the link corresponding to the intended e-mail recipients (Figure 13).
3. Type the e-mail information in the Subject and Message text boxes (Figure 14).
4. Click the Add button to include an attachment.
5. Click the Submit button to complete the process (Figure 15).

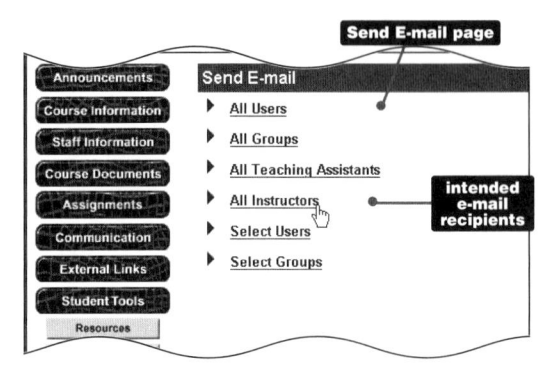

FIGURE 13

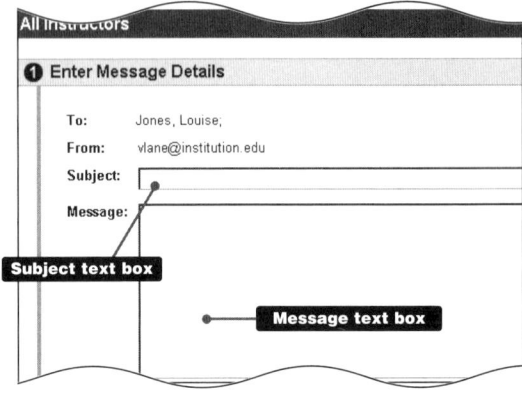

FIGURE 14

A receipt displays to confirm the process. You may continue working on the Send E-mail pages by clicking the OK button or you can return to the course.

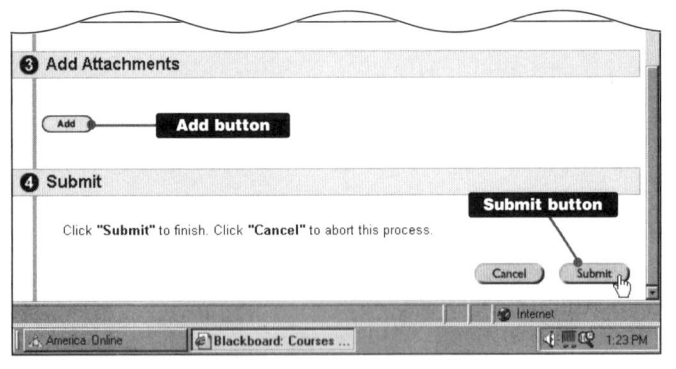

FIGURE 15

Roster

The **Roster** provides a listing of all the students in the class. You can search the roster and view lists of students, instructors, and teaching assistants associated with a particular course. For privacy reasons, you may modify the roster using the Privacy Option.

Viewing the Roster

1. Click the Communication button in the navigation area, and then click Roster (see Figure 12 on the previous page).
2. Click the LIST ALL tab (Figure 16).
3. Click the List All button (Figure 17). A list of currently enrolled students displays (Figure 18).

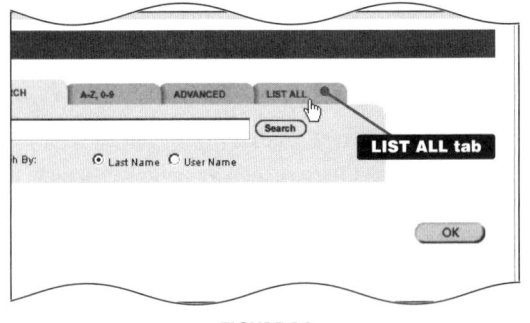

FIGURE 16

COMMUNICATION TOOLS

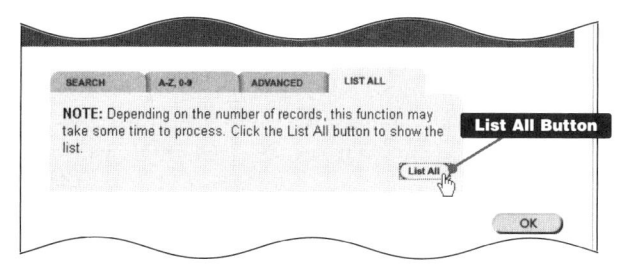

FIGURE 17

4. Click the student's name to view his or her student page.
5. Click the student's e-mail address to send an e-mail. Your default e-mail program will open.

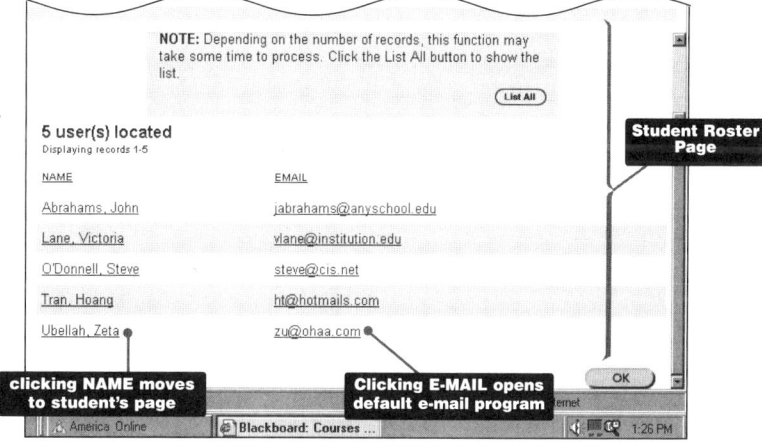

Group Pages

Blackboard allows instructors the ability to divide students into study groups within the **Group Pages** option. Each group will receive a unique group page that provides a list of the group members with a direct access e-mail link. Groups also can use a set of private group tools, including Discussion Board, Virtual Classroom, File Exchange (Drop Box), and E-mail. The instructor will set the parameters for availability. For more information about group pages, refer to the online Student Manual. To view the Student Manual, click Student Tools in the navigation area and then click Manual.

FIGURE 18

Virtual Classroom

Each course includes a synchronous chat room for student and group communications. The chat room is called **Virtual Classroom** and can be used to hold live classroom discussions, TA sessions, and office-hour-type question/answer forums. You also can view previous archived chat sessions within Virtual Classroom.

Entering the Virtual Classroom

1. Click the Communication button in the navigation area.
2. Click Virtual Classroom (see Figure 12 on page 9).

Entering Virtual Classroom

1. Click Enter Virtual Classroom (Figure 19).

Browsing Archives

1. Click Browse Archives (Figure 19).

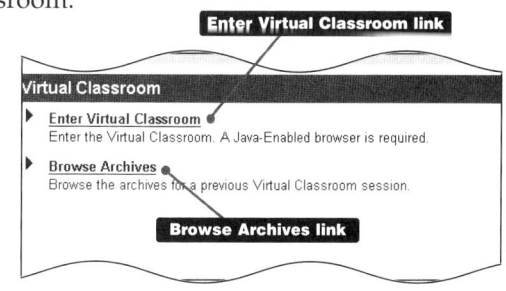

FIGURE 19

STUDENT GUIDE TO BLACKBOARD | 11

COMMUNICATION TOOLS

EXPLORING THE VIRTUAL CLASSROOM   A **Virtual Classroom** consists of a variety of components for working efficiently in the Blackboard environment. Table 2 lists each component of the Virtual Classroom and specifies its function. For more information about the Virtual Classroom, refer to the online Student Manual. To view the Student Manual, click the Student Tools button in the navigation area and then click Manual.

Table 2 Areas of the Virtual Classroom

AREA NAME	FUNCTION
Whiteboard space	Use the whiteboard space (large center area) to display Web pages. You also can write or draw on this space using the Whiteboard toolbar.
Menu items	Use the menu items to change the information that displays on the whiteboard space, such as selecting a font to use on the whiteboard space, moving an object on the whiteboard space behind another object, and moving from one slide on the whiteboard space to another slide.
Location text box	Use the Location text box to enter the URL of a Web page you would like to use in your discussion. The Web page then displays on the whiteboard space. Users also can write or draw on the Web page with the Whiteboard toolbar.
Whiteboard toolbar	Use the Whiteboard toolbar to write and draw on the whiteboard space.
Discussion Tabs	Use the microphone tab to read and add to a discussion, the QA Tab to ask questions of your instructor, the Rotary File tab to view user information, and the Navigate Slides tab to move between slides.

Discussion Board

Blackboard provides a **Discussion Board** as another communication tool to use in a classroom setting. This feature is designed for asynchronous use, so users do not have to be available at the same time to have a conversation. An additional advantage of the discussion board is that user conversations are logged and organized.

ENTERING A DISCUSSION BOARD To utilize the Discussion Board for effective communication within Blackboard, you must first enter the discussion board area. This area contains links to all the discussion boards in the course.

Entering a Discussion Board
1. Click the Communication button in the navigation area.
2. Click Discussion Board (see Figure 12 on page 9).

ADDING A NEW THREAD Conversations are grouped into **forums** that contain threads and all related replies. Your instructor must create a forum in order for you to add a new thread. If the instructor has made this option available, there will be a button that allows you to Add New Thread within a forum.

When adding a new thread, the following options are available: **Smart Text** allows for entry of regular text and for the use of HTML tags. **Plain Text** prevents the rendering of HTML tags. **HTML** interprets the HTML tags present in the text. This function is useful when extensive HTML coding is used within the text.

Adding a New Thread
1. Click the name of the discussion board within which you would like to start a thread of discussion (Figure 20).

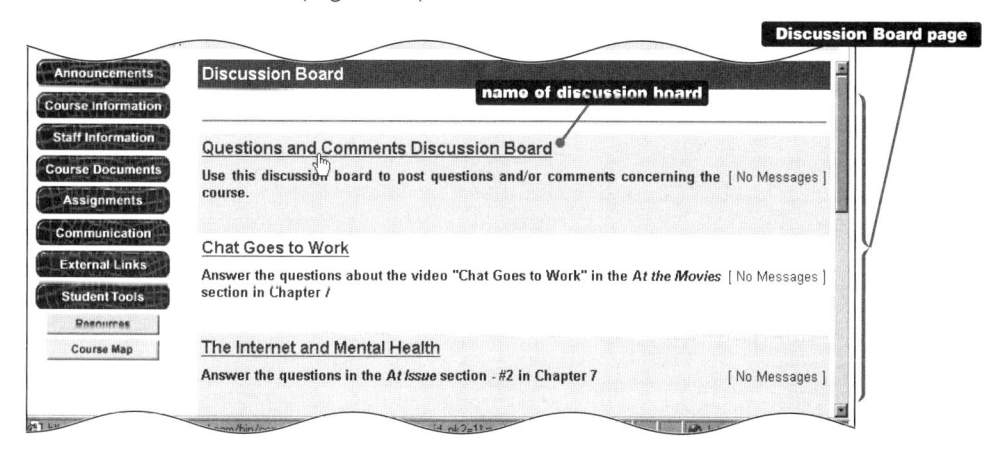

FIGURE 20

2. Click the Add New Thread button (Figure 21).

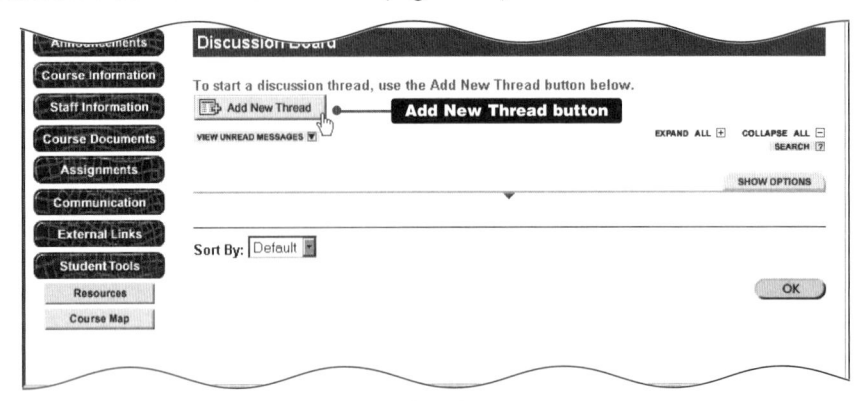

FIGURE 21

3. Type the subject and message to be posted (Figure 22).
4. Click an appropriate option button in the Options area.
5. Click the Preview button to view your message before it is posted.

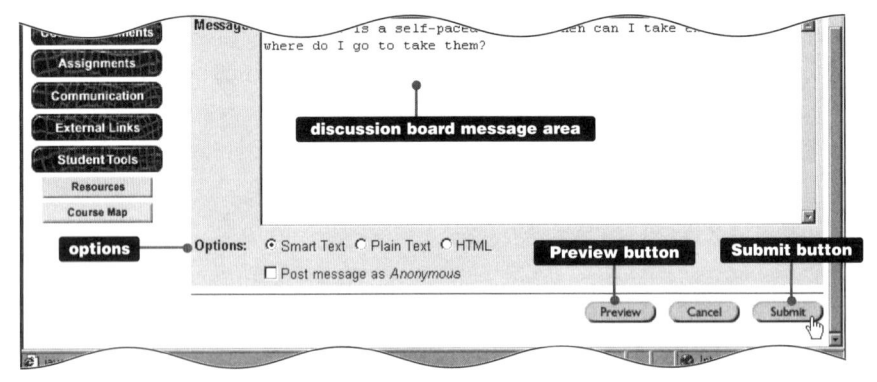

FIGURE 22

6. Click the Submit button to post your message. Your thread will display with a New icon (Figure 23).

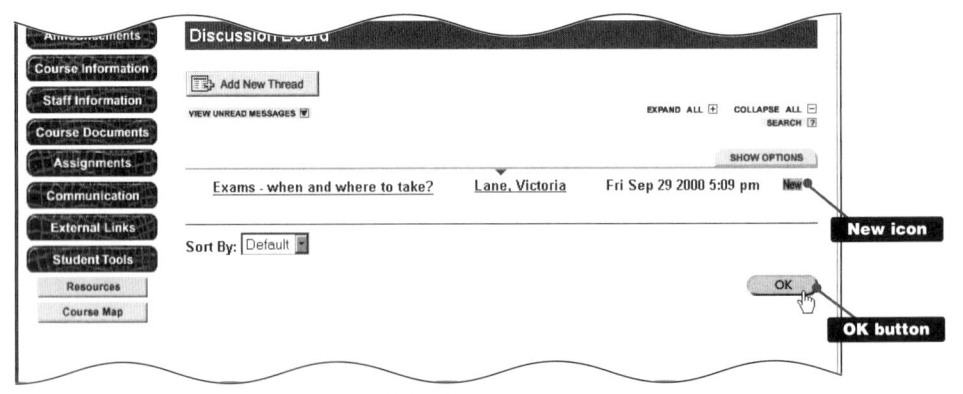

FIGURE 23

COMMUNICATION TOOLS

7. Click the OK button to return to the Discussion Board start page (Figure 23).

READING AND REPLYING TO A MESSAGE While in a discussion group, you will be reading and replying to messages from instructors and classmates.

Reading or Replying to a Message

1. Click the name of the discussion board you would like to enter.
2. Click the name of the message to which you would like to respond (Figure 24).
3. Click the Reply button to post a reply (Figure 25).
4. Type the subject and message to be posted (Figure 26 on the next page).
5. Click the Preview button to view your message before it is posted.
6. Click the Submit button to post your message.

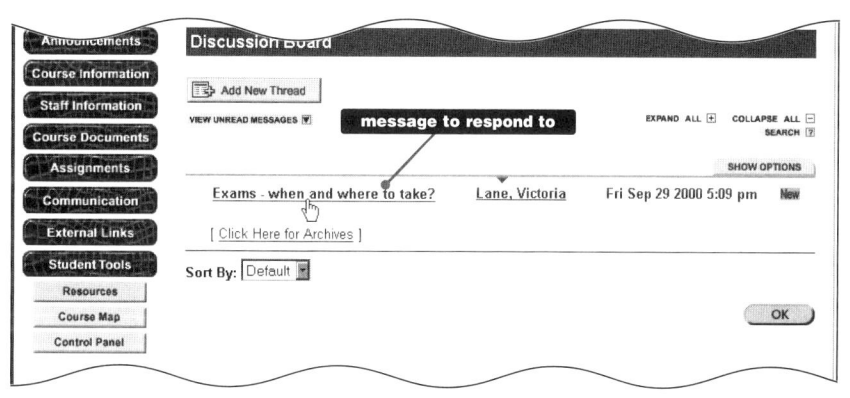

FIGURE 24

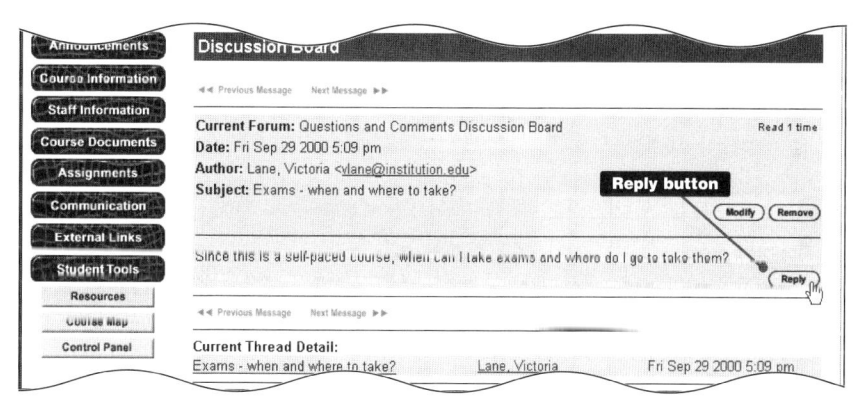

FIGURE 25

STUDENT GUIDE TO BLACKBOARD | 15

COMMUNICATION TOOLS

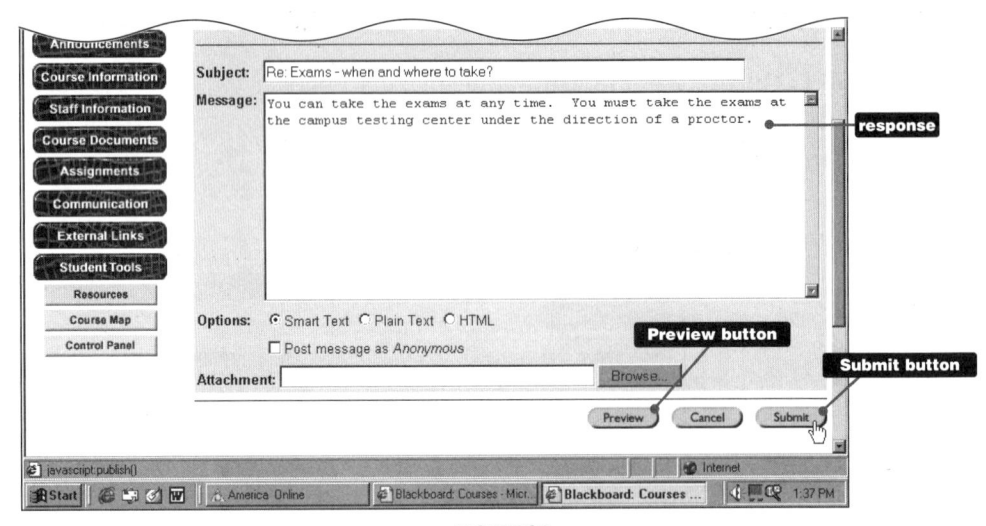

FIGURE 26

The message to which you are responding will display below the text boxes for the reply (Figure 27).

Your message is posted and marked with a New icon (Figure 28).

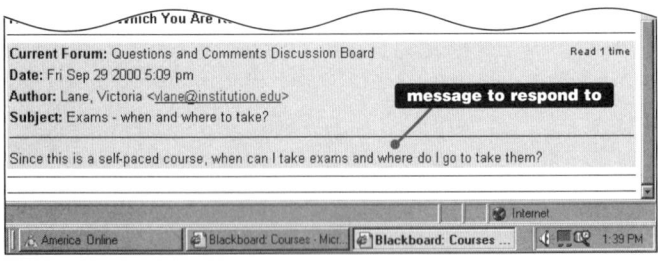

FIGURE 27

DELETING THREADS The instructor will determine whether users will have the ability to modify or remove a posted thread. Consult the instructor of your course to learn user access settings.

EXPANDING AND COLLAPSING MESSAGES When replies are posted to a thread, you have the ability to view the subject line of the replies by clicking the EXPAND ALL box or you can close (hide) all messages added below the original thread by clicking the COLLAPSE ALL box.

If you click the COLLAPSE ALL box, messages added to the original thread will not be displayed (Figure 29).

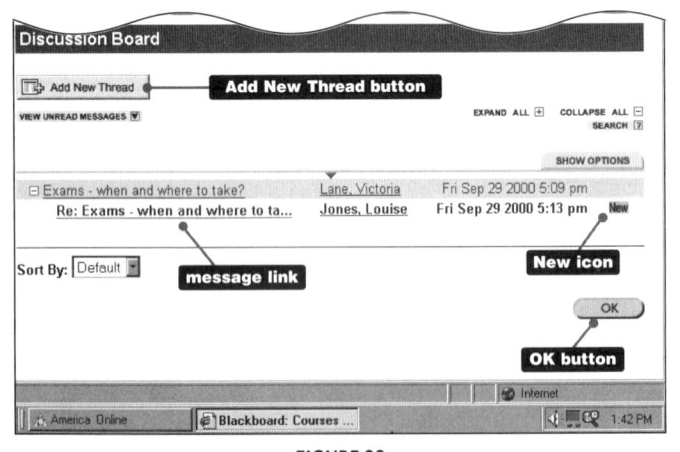

FIGURE 28

16 | STUDENT GUIDE TO BLACKBOARD

COMMUNICATION TOOLS

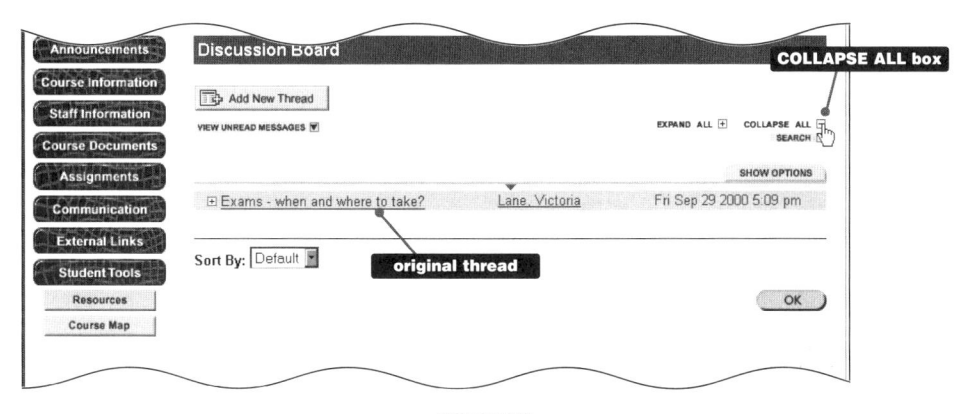

FIGURE 29

If you click the EXPAND ALL box, messages added to the original thread will be displayed below the original thread (Figure 30).

SEARCHING WITHIN A FORUM You have the ability to search for a thread within a specific forum. For example, you may want to view all messages and responses that contain information about exams or you may want to view all messages and responses from just the instructor or from a particular student in the class.

Searching within a Forum

1. Click the SEARCH box (Figure 31).
2. Type the word or phrase to search in the Keywords text box. Or, select a user from the By Author list. Select the appropriate search criteria and then click the Submit button (Figure 32 on the next page).

The search results display. The word or phrase that you typed in the Keywords text box displays in bold (Figure 33 on the next page).

3. Click the OK button to return to the thread view.

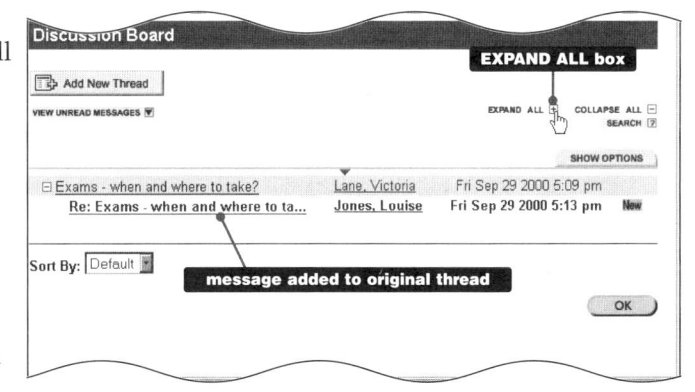

FIGURE 30

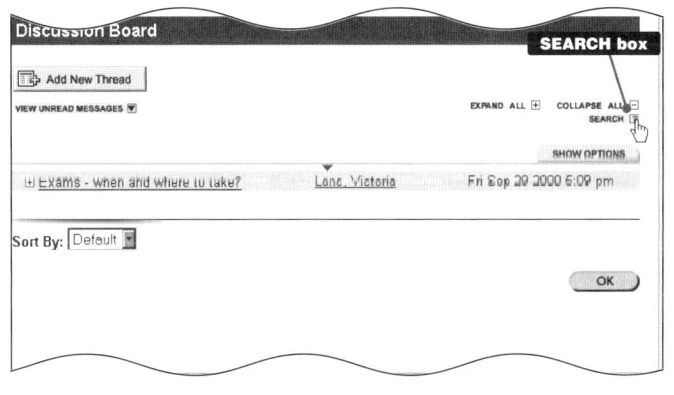

FIGURE 31

STUDENT GUIDE TO BLACKBOARD | 17

COMMUNICATION TOOLS

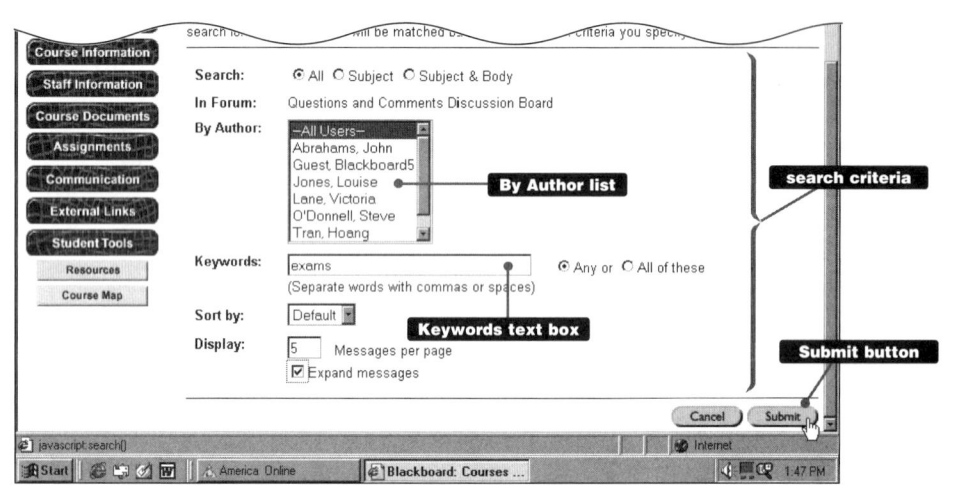

FIGURE 32

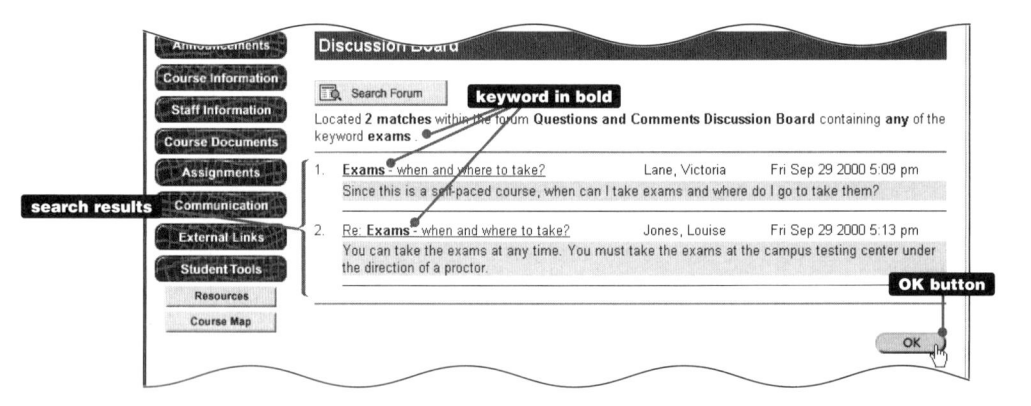

FIGURE 33

SHOWING AND MODIFYING THREAD OPTIONS You have the ability to manipulate your view of threads by utilizing the thread options.

Using Thread Options

1. Click the SHOW OPTIONS tab (Figure 34).

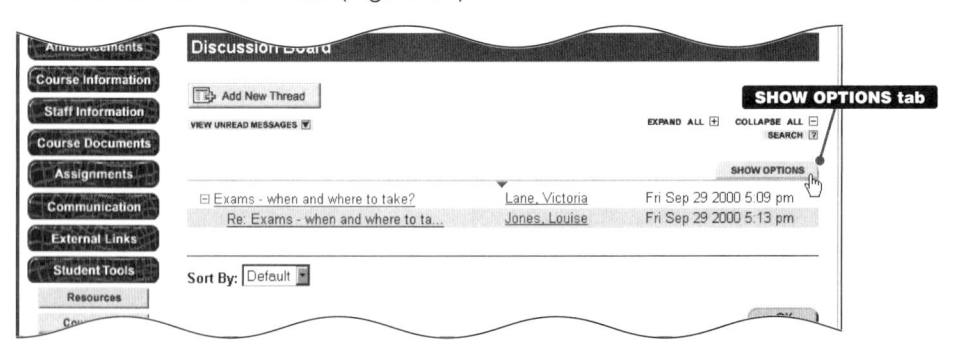

FIGURE 34

COMMUNICATION TOOLS

2. When the thread options display, select the thread option of your choice (Figure 35). The tab changes from SHOW OPTIONS to HIDE OPTIONS.

Table 3 lists each thread option and specifies its function.

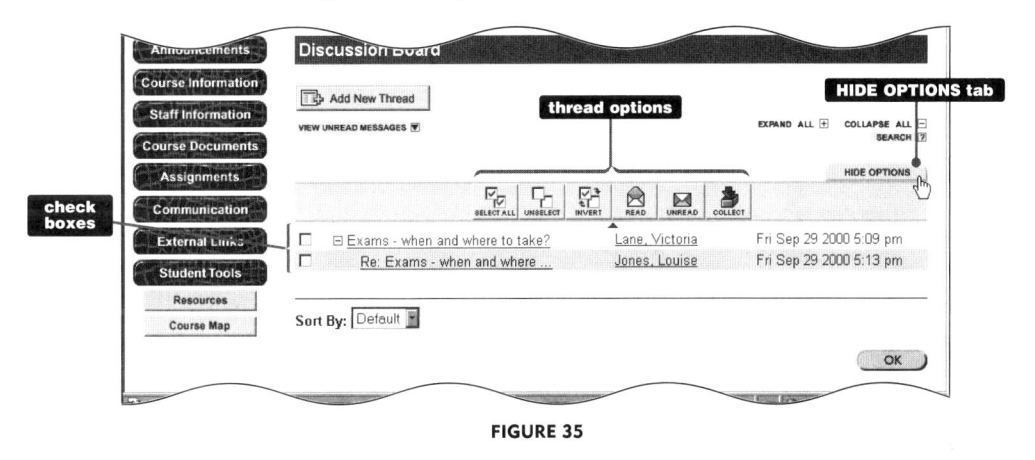

FIGURE 35

Table 3 Thread Options

THREAD OPTION	FUNCTION
SELECT ALL	Places a check in the check box of all the messages listed within the discussion board.
UNSELECT	Remove the check mark from all of the selected items.
INVERT	Inverts your previous selection. For example, if you previously clicked Select All, you can click Invert to Unselect All.
READ	Marks a message as read, removing the New icon. You can execute this by clicking the check box of the desired message.
UNREAD	Marks a message as unread, adding the New icon. You can execute this by clicking the check box of the desired message.
COLLECT	Collects all of the messages you want to view and then displays them on one page. You can execute this by clicking the check box of the desired message(s).

Modifying Thread Options

1. Click the check boxes next to the messages you would like to modify.
2. Click the name of the option you would like to perform and the function will take effect (Figure 35).

STUDENT GUIDE TO BLACKBOARD | 19

STUDENT TOOLS

SORTING You can modify the message display by using the Sort By list to modify the message display using a specified criteria.

Sorting by Criteria
1. Click the Sort By box arrow to display a list of viewing criteria.
2. Click the desired viewing criteria in the Sort By list (Figure 36).

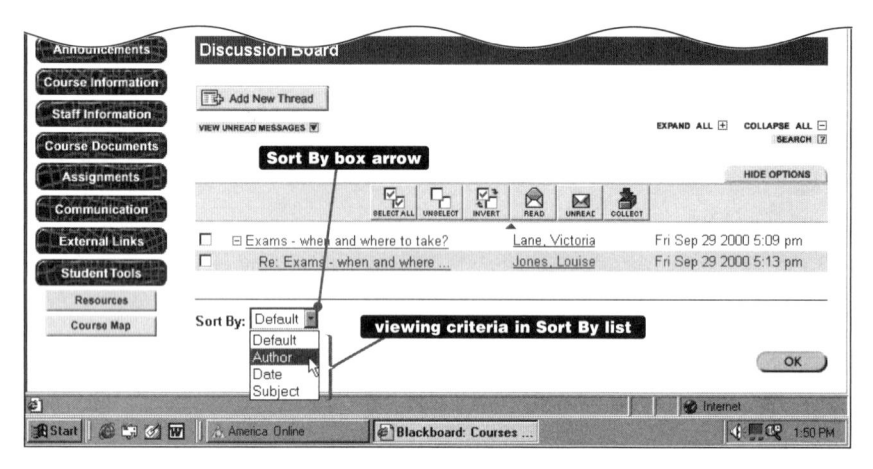

FIGURE 36

STUDENT TOOLS

Blackboard provides many tools students can use to manage course materials, track course dates, and customize user items (Figure 37 and Figure 38).

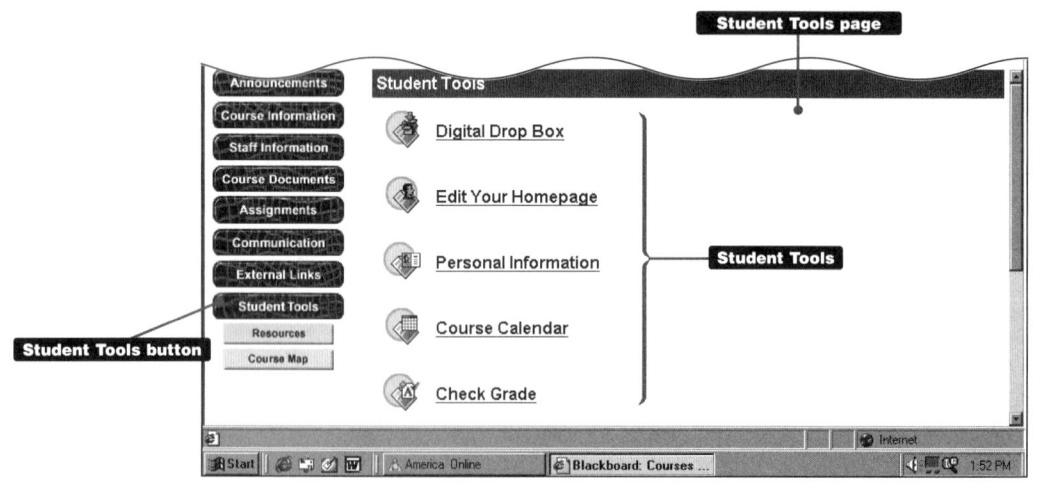

FIGURE 37

STUDENT TOOLS

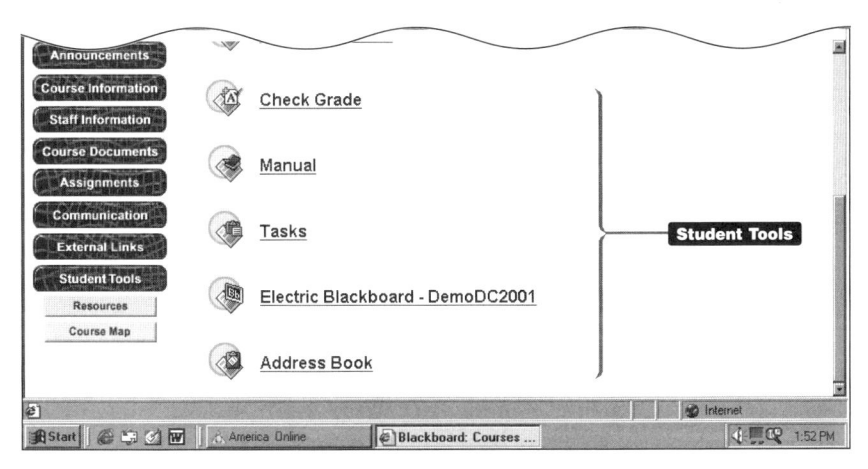

FIGURE 38

Digital Drop Box

The **Drop Box** is a tool that instructors and students can use to exchange files (reports, papers, etc.) by uploading a file from a disk or a computer to a central location. A student or instructor can then download the document onto his or her system. Students can access the Drop Box from the Student Tools page. The Drop Box allows students and instructors to share files. Students also have access to a group Drop Box if instructors have designated study groups with this option enabled. For more information on groups, refer to the online Student Manual. To view the Student Manual, click Student Tools in the navigation area and then click Manual.

The **Student Drop Box** is used to exchange materials between a single student and the instructor. The **Group Drop Box** is used to exchange materials between group members. Information that needs to be posted for all students should be placed in the Discussion Board.

Sending a File to the Digital Drop Box

1. Click the Student Tools button in the navigation area and then click Digital Drop Box (see Figure 37).
2. Click the Send File button (Figure 39).

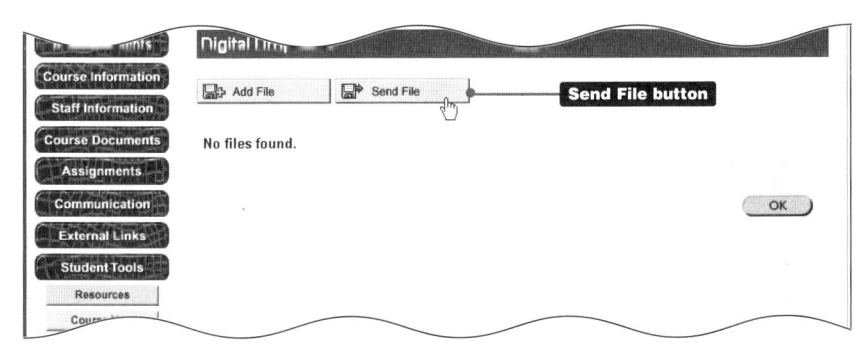

FIGURE 39

STUDENT TOOLS

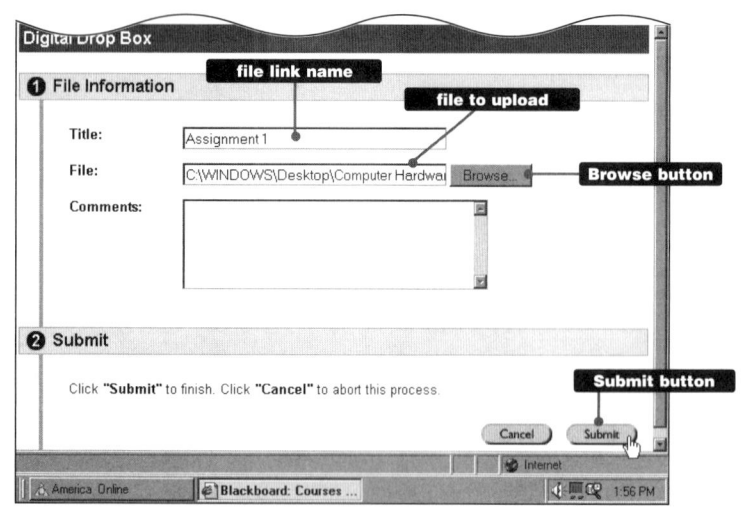

FIGURE 40

3. Indicate a File to upload by clicking the Browse button and selecting the appropriate file.
4. Type the text to display with the file link name in the Title text box.
5. Click the Submit button to send the file to the Drop Box where it can be accessed by your instructor (Figure 40).
6. After the receipt displays, click the OK button to continue working in the Drop Box or return to the course by clicking the appropriate button in the navigation area.

Downloading a File from the Digital Drop Box

1. Click the Student Tools button in the navigation area and then click Digital Drop Box (see Figure 37 on page 20). The Digital Drop Box page displays a list of the files available to download.
2. Right-click the link for the file (command click for MAC users), and then click Save Target As on the shortcut menu (Figure 41).
3. Save the file to an appropriate location.

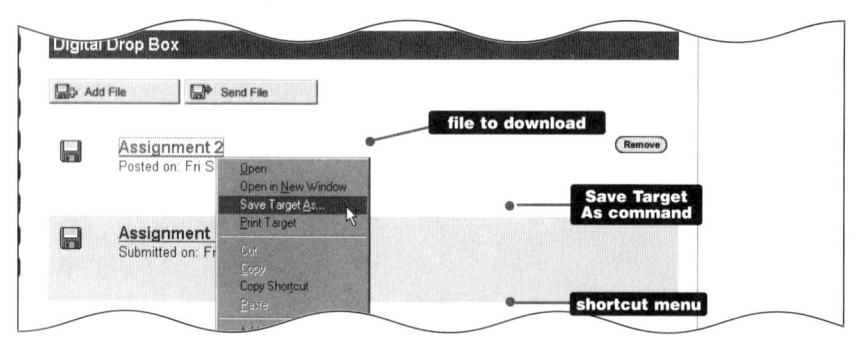

FIGURE 41

Deleting a File from the Digital Drop Box

This option is visible only if the instructor makes it available to the student.

1. When a file is no longer needed, click the Student Tools button and then click Digital Drop Box (see Figure 37 on page 20).
2. Click the Remove button next to the file you want to delete (Figure 42).
3. When the warning dialog box displays, click the OK button. A receipt displays.

STUDENT TOOLS

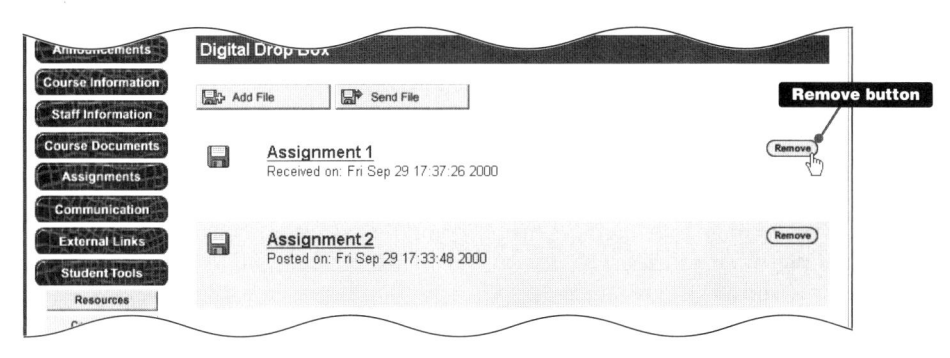

FIGURE 42

4. Click the OK button to continue working in the Digital Drop Box, or return to the course by clicking the appropriate button in the navigation area.

Edit Your Homepage

You can create a unique **student homepage**, accessible only to other registered participants in your course. You can customize your page by providing some personal information, adding a picture, and listing your favorite Web sites. You also can add HTML to enhance your homepage.

Editing Your Homepage

1. Click the Student Tools button in the navigation area and then click Edit Your Homepage (see Figure 37 on page 20).
2. Type an introduction in the Intro Message text box and add some personal information in the Personal Information text box (Figure 43). Use HTML if you desire.
3. Click the Browse button to upload a picture of yourself, and then locate the file from your directories (Figure 44)
4. Enter up to three of your favorite Web sites by filling in the appropriate text boxes in the Favorite Web Sites area (Figure 45 on the next page).
5. Click the Submit button to enter your changes (Figure 45).
6. View your homepage by clicking the Communication button in the navigation area and clicking Roster (see Figure 12 on page 9).

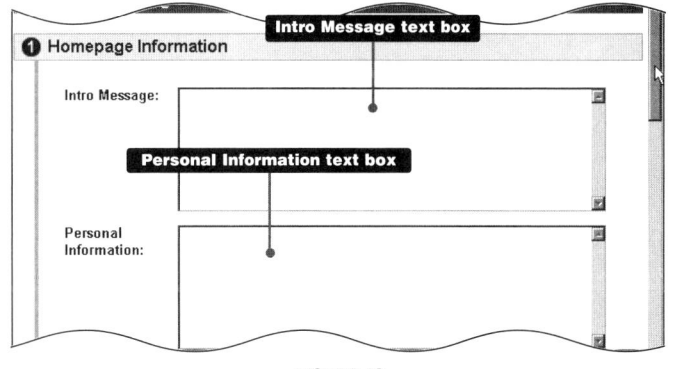

FIGURE 43

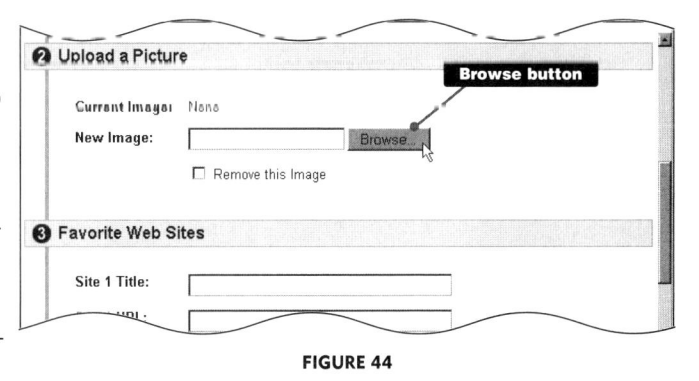

FIGURE 44

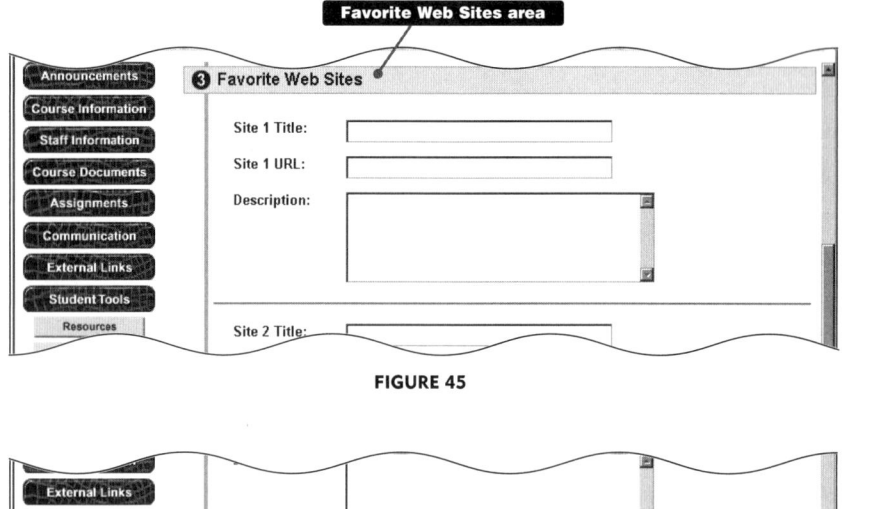

STUDENT TOOLS

FIGURE 45

FIGURE 46

7. Follow the Viewing the Roster procedure on pages 10 and 11 in this manual to view your homepage.

Personal Information

Your personal information can be changed anytime using the **Personal Information** area under Student Tools. If at any point during the course of the semester you need to update or modify this information, you can do so within the Personal Information area. Consider using this tool when you get a new e-mail address, move, or get a new telephone number.

You also can use it to change your password at anytime, set the CD-ROM drive to access content on your local computer, and select which fields of your contact information will be publicly available

Editing Personal Information

1. Click the Student Tools button in the navigation area and then click Personal Information (see Figure 37 on page 20).
2. Click Edit Personal Information (Figure 47).
3. Scroll to the field you want to change and type the new information (Figure 48).

STUDENT TOOLS

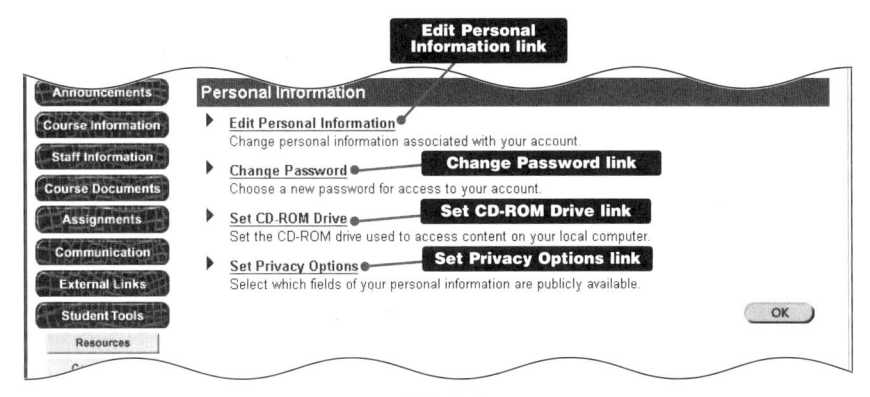

FIGURE 47

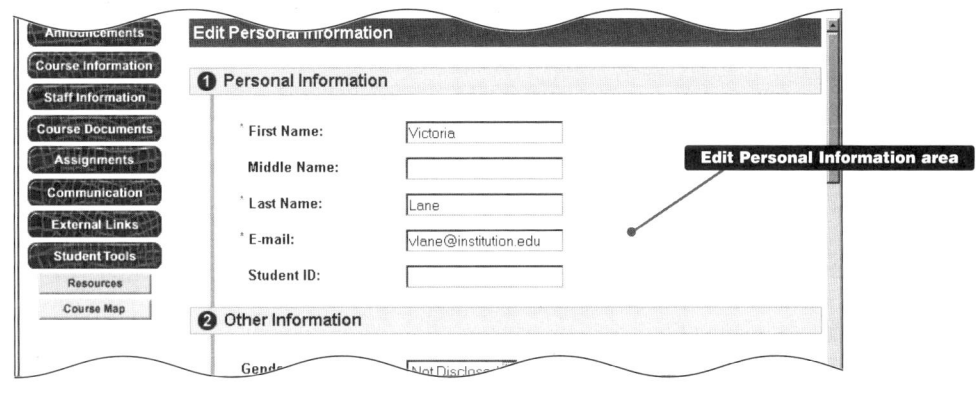

FIGURE 48

4. Click the Submit button (Figure 49).

The Edit Personal Information tool updates your student record in the system. Accordingly, your student record in other courses will update automatically.

Changing Your Password

1. Click the Student Tools button and then click Personal Information (see Figure 37 on page 20).
2. Click Change Password (Figure 47).
3. Type a new password.
4. Type the new password a second time for verification.
5. Click the Submit button (Figure 50 on the next page).

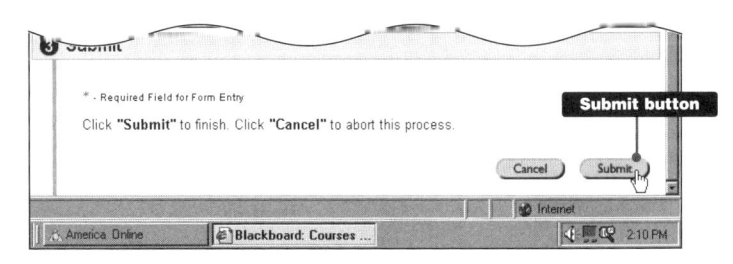

FIGURE 49

STUDENT GUIDE TO BLACKBOARD | 25

STUDENT TOOLS

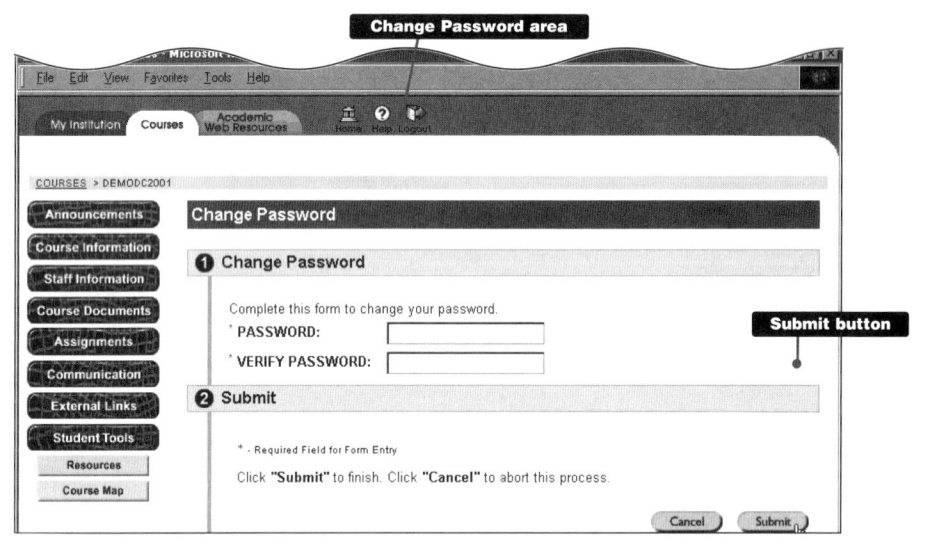

FIGURE 50

The Edit Personal Information tool updates your password in the system. Accordingly, your password in other courses will update automatically.

Setting Your CD-ROM Drive

1. Click the Student Tools button in the navigation area and then click Personal Information (see Figure 37 on page 20).
2. Click Set CD-ROM Drive (see Figure 47 on the previous page).
3. Click the CD-ROM (for PC) box arrow and then click a letter for your CD-ROM drive in the list or type in the appropriate CD-ROM drive location in the CD-ROM (for MAC) text box.
4. Click the Submit button (Figure 51).

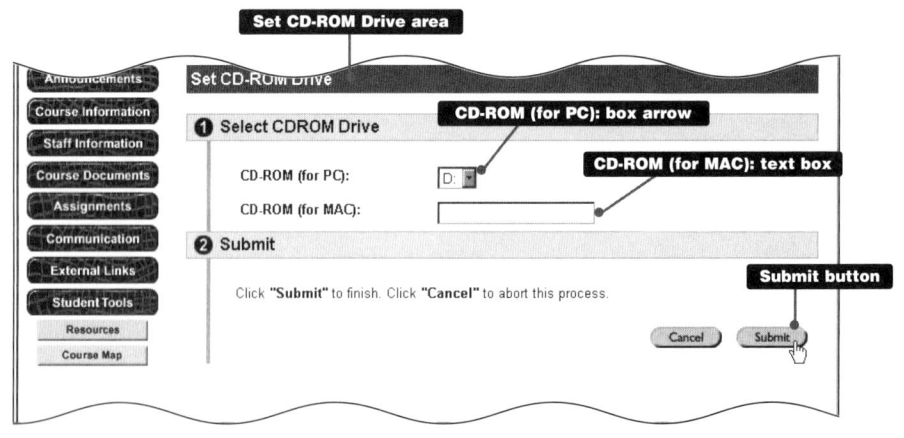

FIGURE 51

26 | STUDENT GUIDE TO BLACKBOARD

Setting Privacy Options

1. Click the Student Tools button in the navigation area and then click Personal Information (see Figure 37 on page 20).
2. Click Set Privacy Options (see Figure 47 on page 25).
3. Select one or more check boxes to include the corresponding information in your user profile (Figure 52).
4. Click the Submit button (Figure 53).

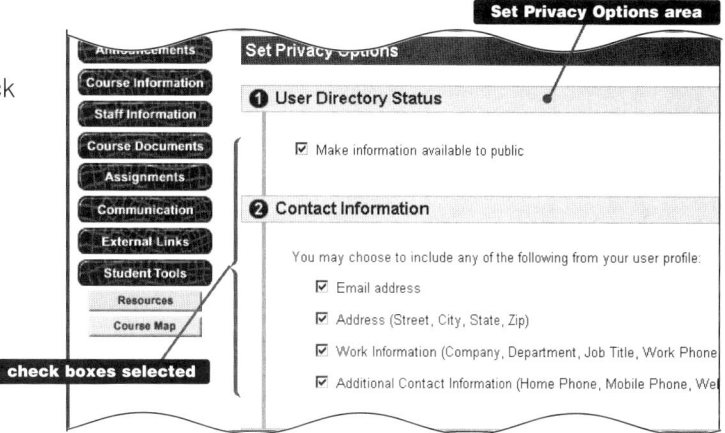

FIGURE 52

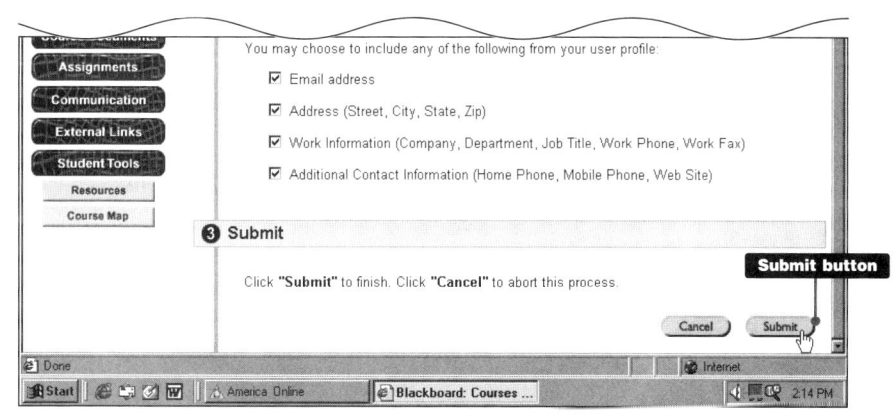

FIGURE 53

Course Calendar

Blackboard provides a **Course Calendar** you can use to track important course- and campus-related events. You can view the calendar events that are posted in the current course in Student Tools.

Viewing the Calendar

1. Click the Student Tools button and then click Course Calendar (see Figure 37 on page 20).

CALENDAR VIEWS You can view events in the Course Calendar in a number of views. To view calendar events, click the desired calendar view tab. The Calendar start page automatically defaults to View Day.

VIEW DAY: **View Day** displays the current day. You can click the arrows on either side of the date in View Day to move between days (see Figure 54 on the next page).

STUDENT TOOLS

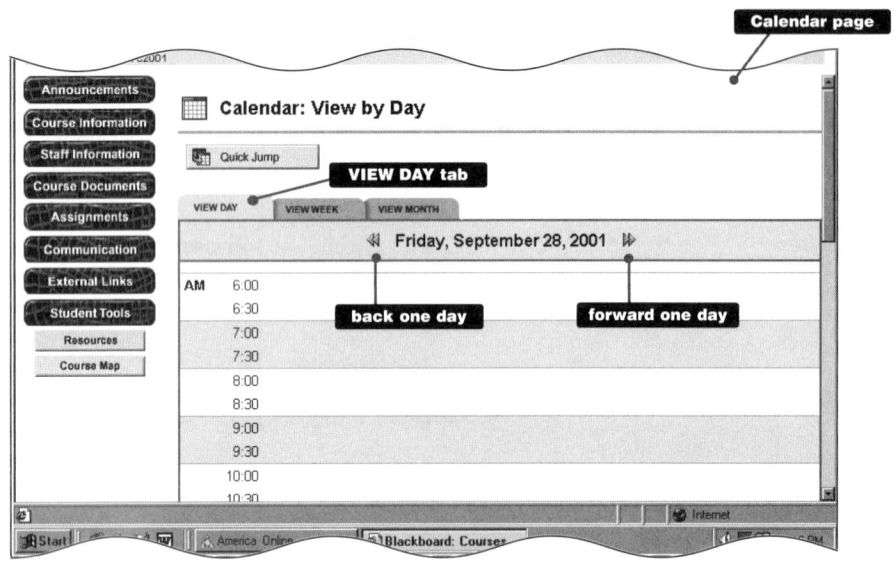

FIGURE 54

VIEW WEEK: **View Week** displays the events scheduled for a week, listing each event title and time below the corresponding day. You can click the arrows on either side of the week in View Week to move between weeks (Figure 55).

VIEW MONTH: **View Month** displays the scheduled events for an entire month, sectioned by day. You can click the arrows on either side of the month in View Month to move between months (Figure 56).

QUICK JUMP: **Quick Jump** allows you to view past and future calendar events. You are required to supply the information that will jump to the desired calendar event.

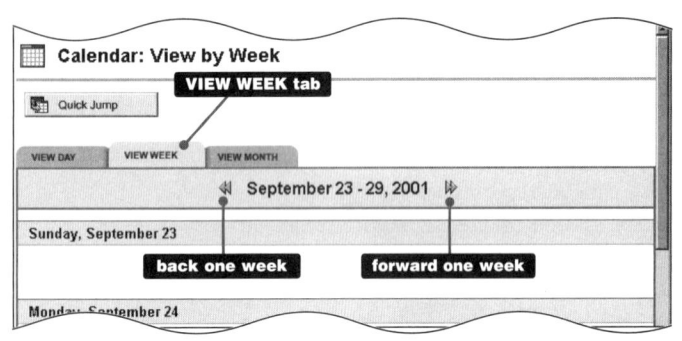

FIGURE 55

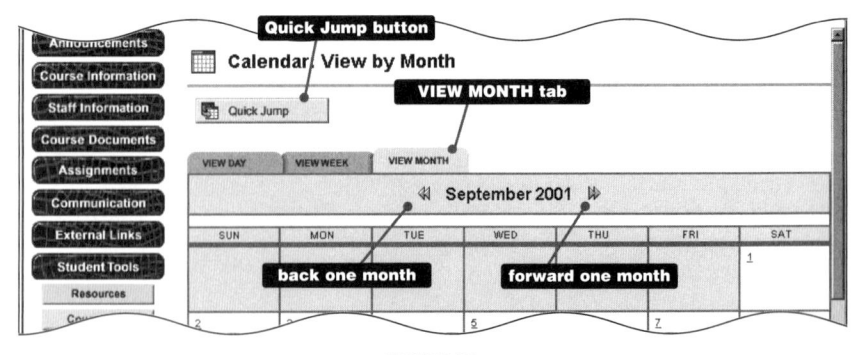

FIGURE 56

STUDENT TOOLS

Quick Jump to a Future or Past Date on the Calendar
1. Click the Quick Jump button (Figure 56).
2. Select date and type of view criteria.
3. Click the Submit button (Figure 57).

Check Grade
If the instructor permits student access, you can check your grades at anytime with the **Check Grade** tool.

Viewing Your Grades
1. Click the Student Tools button and then click Check Grade (see Figure 37 on page 20).

The student grades display in a similar format to the format shown in Figure 58, but will contain items appropriate to your course as entered by your instructor.

2. To view a specific Quiz/Exam result, click the Quiz/Exam score.

FIGURE 57

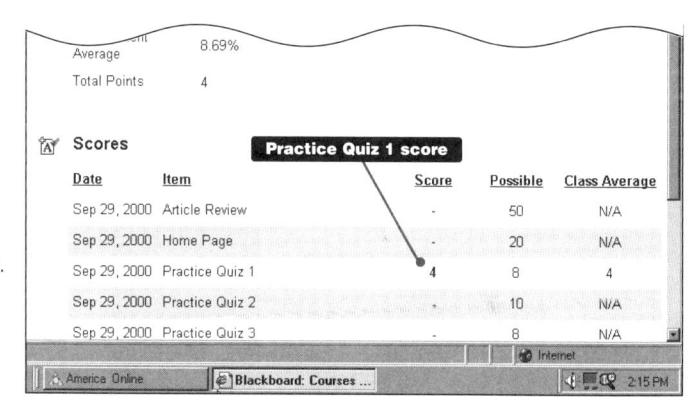

FIGURE 58

Manual
In addition to the bound *Student Guide to Blackboard*, an online Student Manual is available within the Student Tools area for your convenience.

Viewing the Student Manual
1. Click the Student Tools button in the navigation area.
2. Click Manual (see Figure 38 on page 21).

Using the Student Manual online allows you to search for specific areas while in the Blackboard course, as well as providing a useful online reference for the course.

Tasks
The Tasks page organizes projects, defines task priority, and tracks task status. Task information is arranged in columns that display the priority, task name, status, and due date. Tasks are assigned by the instructor and relate to the activities in the course.

STUDENT GUIDE TO BLACKBOARD | 29

STUDENT TOOLS

Viewing Tasks

1. Click the Student Tools button in the navigation area and then click Tasks (see Figure 38 on page 21).
2. View the Tasks page (Figure 59).

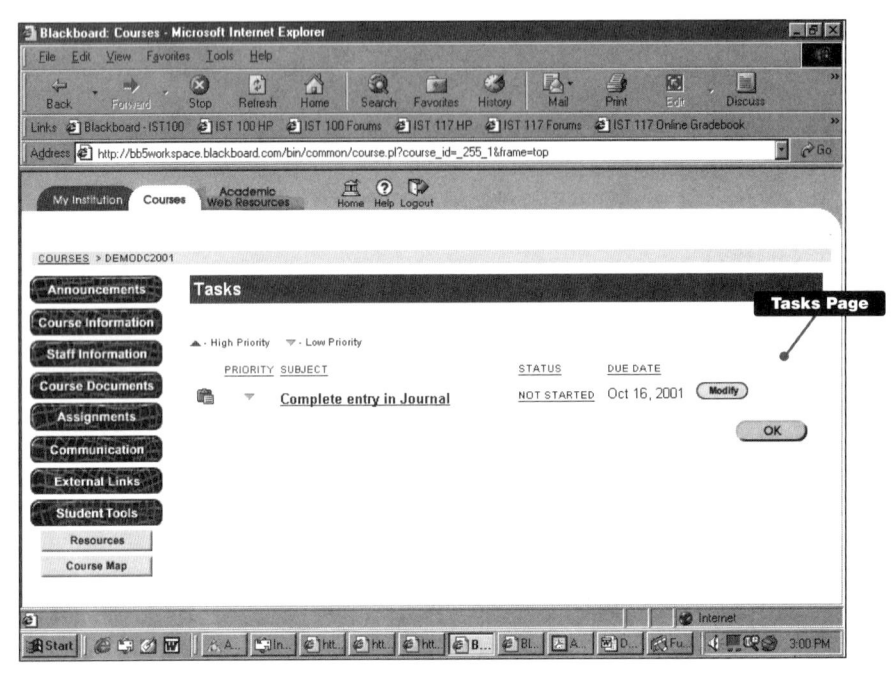

FIGURE 59

Students can view the details of a particular task but are limited to modifying the task priority and task status. For more information about viewing and modifying tasks, refer to the online Student Manual. To view the Student Manual, click Student Tools in the navigation area and then click Manual.

Electric Blackboard

The Electric Blackboard allows users to save notes for a particular course within the Blackboard 5 environment.

Viewing the Electric Blackboard

1. Click the Student Tools button in the navigation area and then click Electric Blackboard (see Figure 38 on page 21).
2. Type any notes in the large white area that you wish to save.
3. Click the Submit button to save the notes (Figure 60).

STUDENT TOOLS

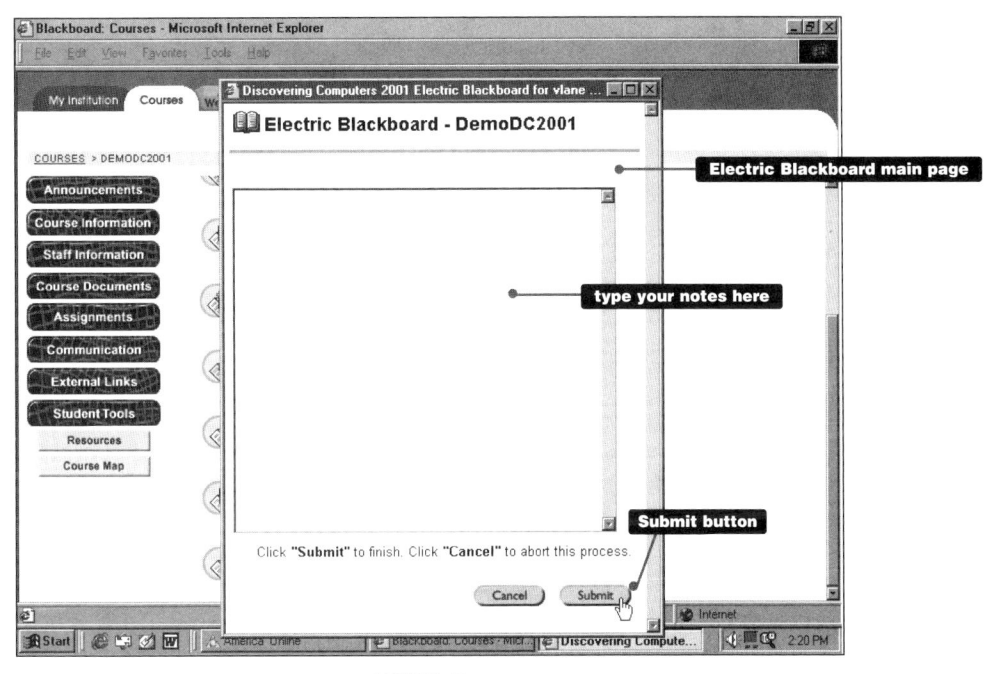

FIGURE 60

Address Book

Users store the information for personal contact using the Address Book. To add a contact the user must enter in a profile for anyone they wish to add to their address book. The Address Book also contains a search function at the top of the page. Users can search using different variables selected from the search tabs.

Viewing the Address Book

1. Click the Student Tools button in the navigation area and then click Address Book (see Figure 38 on page 21).
2. View the Address Book page (Figure 61).

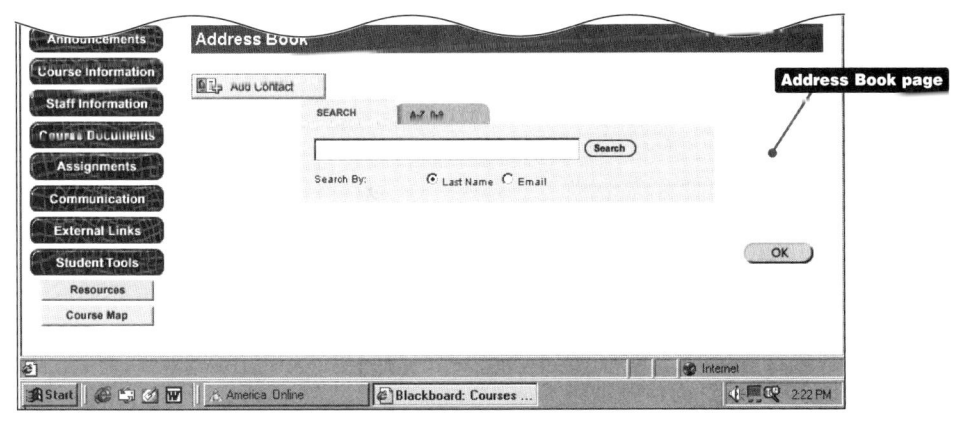

FIGURE 61

STUDENT GUIDE TO BLACKBOARD | 31

For more information about adding and displaying contacts, refer to the online Student Manual. To view the Student Manual, click Student Tools in the navigation area and then click Manual.

SUCCESSFUL USE OF THE STUDENT GUIDE TO BLACKBOARD

As a valuable tool in your academic success, using the *Student Guide to Blackboard* has directed you through the navigation, features, and functionality of your Blackboard course. After reading this manual, you now are able to navigate in a course and access course materials. You know how to send e-mail, create and edit individual student and group pages, display a student roster, and participate in both synchronous and asynchronous discussions. In addition, you are prepared to send and receive file attachments, change your personal information at anytime, check your grades in the course, and view the course calendar. For more information on Blackboard, contact Blackboard on the Web at www.blackboard.com or by mail at 1899 L Street, NW, 5th Floor, Washington, DC 20036.